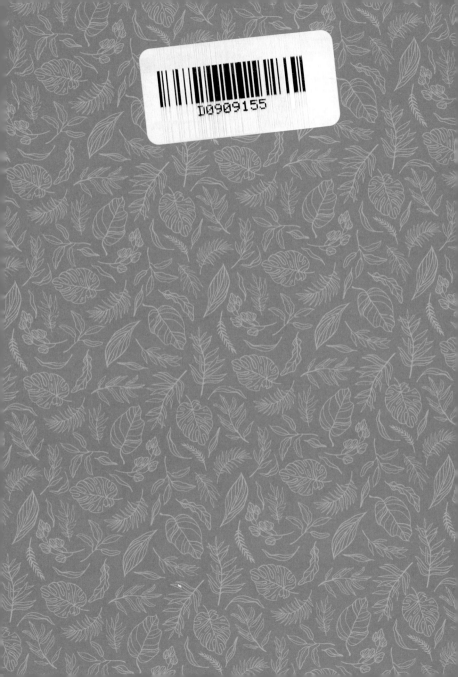

TO

_____

FROM

_____

DATE

_____

worthy

50 Mindful Moments

to Bring Clarity and Peace

to Your Day

BRITTNEY MOSES

LIVE YOUR FAITH

Written by: Brittney Moses
Cover Design by: Jessica Wei

Printed in China
Prime: J8529
ISBN: 978-1-64870-796-4

contents

introduction

When reflecting on all the ideas I could've written about around faith and mental health I became more and more convinced that lately many of us were simply in need of a mental break. With the over-saturation of media and rush of today's cultural demands, I wanted to create something that was refreshing to read, honest, faith-inspired and integrated with psychological tips and insights to get clear about how you're showing up for your life each day.

The more I have the honor of walking alongside the stories of others, the more I get to see how truly similar we are, even in the thoughts that we feel are too overwhelming to handle or too shameful to say out loud. We are more tethered to one another through the human experience than we may realize. Still by the grace of God, we are capable of showing up wholeheartedly to the lives we've been called to lead.

When people ask about the work and advocacy I do around mental health, I've come to realize that my academic studies, research and crisis training helped give me the language and practical tools, but it's my personal experiences both within myself and those around me that have helped give me understanding. Together I hope to bring a wholesome approach to this book which has truly been a labor of love. From my heart to yours.

With love,

Brittney Moses

enter your day with intention

For you formed my inward parts;
you knitted me together in my mother's womb.

PSALM 139:13 ESV

In this moment, the breath that rises and falls inside your lungs, the blood that courses through your veins, and the heart that pulses against your chest are all signs that your body is awake and you are alive. Through the waves of pressure you thought might overtake you, you are here and very much alive. The constant rhythm of your body is a reminder of this innate resilience.

When we think about our bodies and the intricacies of how we function, from the networking of our brains to the design of the tiniest cell, we get the picture that our Creator is in the details. That every part of us is worthy of our attention.

Still, it can be all too easy to disconnect from God and ourselves when we've been pulled into the demands of the day. So give yourself permission to pause in this moment to reconnect with your breath and realign with your priorities and convictions. What matters most today? How do you want to move through this day? Is it from a more grounded place? A more focused place? Visualize it and reflect on what boundaries will be necessary to live this out today.

Every part of me is worthy of attention.

HOW AM I FEELING TODAY?

☐ **1** Awful   ☐ **2** Poor   ☐ **3** Okay   ☐ **4** Good   ☐ **5** Great

LABELING:

Calm ————————————————————————— Anxious

Motivated ——————————————————————— Unmotivated

Loved ——————————————————————————Lonely

Happy———————————————————————————— Sad

Focused———————————————————————————Distracted

Grateful———————————————————————————— Angry

HOURS OF SLEEP:

☐ 0 – 3   ☐ 4 – 6   ☐ 7 – 9   ☐ 10 – 12   ☐ 13+

EXERCISE: ☐ Yes   ☐ No

TOP 3 GOALS FOR TODAY:

1._____
2._____
3._____

3 THINGS I AM GRATEFUL FOR TODAY:

1._____
2._____
3._____

ONE PRACTICAL WAY I CAN APPLY TODAY'S READING:

_____
_____
_____
_____
_____
_____

the peace of
walking in truth

*Give careful thought to the paths for your feet
and be steadfast in all your ways.*

PROVERBS 4:26 NIV

When we're not living out our values, it creates a discomfort within our minds and spirits called *cognitive dissonance*. *Cognitive* refers to our mental process, and *dissonance* means there's a misalignment. So cognitive dissonance is when our actions aren't aligned with our true convictions and priorities, which creates an unsettledness within us. This unsettledness is the perfect setup for insecurity and anxiety to surface because we're double-minded.

Even though we believe our family should be priority, we're letting other demands crowd them out. We know we're responsible for something, but we avoid it. We say yes to things when deep down we know we're overextended. We constantly compromise our convictions, and this inconsistency weighs on our subconsciouses.

On the outside we seem productive and maybe even likable, but on the inside, we're disconnected from our true selves. We're too consumed with appeasing everyone else and at a loss of how God is calling us to show up for our own lives. My friend, that's just no way to live. We have to be honest with ourselves and those around us to reclaim a life that's grounded in integrity, helping us walk in peace. Where do you need to realign your actions with your values today?

At any moment,
I can realign
my priorities and
convictions to
live true to what
I believe.

DATE:_____

HOW AM I FEELING TODAY?

☐ **1** Awful ☐ **2** Poor ☐ **3** Okay ☐ **4** Good ☐ **5** Great

LABELING:

Calm ——————————————————————————— Anxious

Motivated —————————————————————————— Unmotivated

Loved ————————————————————————————Lonely

Happy———————————————————————— Sad

Focused———————————————————————————Distracted

Grateful———————————————————————————— Angry

HOURS OF SLEEP:

☐ 0 – 3 ☐ 4 – 6 ☐ 7 – 9 ☐ 10 – 12 ☐ 13+

EXERCISE: ☐ Yes ☐ No

TOP 3 GOALS FOR TODAY:

1._____
2._____
3._____

3 THINGS I AM GRATEFUL FOR TODAY:

1._____
2._____
3._____

ONE PRACTICAL WAY I CAN APPLY TODAY'S READING:

_____
_____
_____
_____
_____
_____

living in the freedom of joy

*May the God of hope fill you with all joy and
peace as you trust in Him, so that you may overflow
with hope by the power of the Holy Spirit.*

ROMANS 15:13 NIV

When was the last time you let yourself feel the fullness of joy? The common issue with anxiety is that we convince ourselves to fear things that either haven't happened or don't exist. Sometimes it's so bad that we won't allow ourselves to get too happy, enjoy ourselves too much, or experience the fullness of a great relationship. We're untrusting of anything too good.

But the truth is that you can't experience the fullness of joy without allowing yourself to be vulnerable to the present. Hebrews 11:1 (ESV) reminds us that faith is "the assurance of things hoped for." The very essence of faith is counterintuitive because instead of seeing and then trusting, it is trusting and then seeing. But it is also experiencing the good because *you are trusting* and open to seeing it. I believe joy works in the same way. This doesn't mean that we don't use wisdom and discernment while stepping into the unknown. You are adaptable and resilient should you need to be.

In the meantime, repeat this with me: I am worthy of allowing joy into my life.

Dedicate yourself to one thing that brings you joy this week.

I am worthy of allowing joy into my life.

HOW AM I FEELING TODAY?

☐ **1** Awful   ☐ **2** Poor   ☐ **3** Okay   ☐ **4** Good   ☐ **5** Great

LABELING:

Calm ———————————————————————————— Anxious

Motivated —————————————————————————— Unmotivated

Loved ——————————————————————————————Lonely

Happy—————————————————————————————— Sad

Focused——————————————————————————————Distracted

Grateful————————————————————————————— Angry

HOURS OF SLEEP:

☐ 0 – 3   ☐ 4 – 6   ☐ 7 – 9   ☐ 10 – 12   ☐ 13+

EXERCISE: ☐ Yes   ☐ No

TOP 3 GOALS FOR TODAY:

1. _____
2. _____
3. _____

3 THINGS I AM GRATEFUL FOR TODAY:

1. _____
2. _____
3. _____

ONE PRACTICAL WAY I CAN APPLY TODAY'S READING:

_____
_____
_____
_____
_____
_____

taking every thought captive

You will keep in perfect peace
those whose minds are steadfast,
because they trust in You.

ISAIAH 26:3 NIV

One of the beautiful complexities that is woven into the human mind is this superpower called metacognition. *Metacognition* is your ability to *think* about your thoughts. This means that you can separate yourself long enough to examine your own thoughts. And if you can think outside of your thoughts, this is proof that *you are not your thoughts*.

Just because a thought exists doesn't automatically make it true. At any moment, you have the ability to take a step back and choose between which thoughts you will align yourself with and which you'll reject. It's this very process of metacognition that allows us to "take every thought captive to obey Christ" (II Corinthians 10:5 ESV).

How you feel about yourself or your circumstance today doesn't change God's call over your life. If a thought doesn't align with who God created you to be—loved, forgiven, redeemed, secure, full of purpose, made for good works—then it is the *thought* that is flawed. It is the thought that needs to be changed and brought into alignment with the truth that never changed. In Christ, we're no longer striving *for* worth but living *from* worth. Rest in this today.

Just because a thought exists doesn't automatically make it true.

HOW AM I FEELING TODAY?

☐ **1** Awful   ☐ **2** Poor   ☐ **3** Okay   ☐ **4** Good   ☐ **5** Great

LABELING:

Calm ———————————————————————— Anxious

Motivated ————————————————————— Unmotivated

Loved ————————————————————————Lonely

Happy———————————————————————— Sad

Focused————————————————————————Distracted

Grateful———————————————————————— Angry

HOURS OF SLEEP:

☐ 0 – 3   ☐ 4 – 6   ☐ 7 – 9   ☐ 10 – 12   ☐ 13+

EXERCISE: ☐ Yes   ☐ No

TOP 3 GOALS FOR TODAY:

1._____
2._____
3._____

3 THINGS I AM GRATEFUL FOR TODAY:

1._____
2._____
3._____

ONE PRACTICAL WAY I CAN APPLY TODAY'S READING:

_____
_____
_____
_____
_____
_____

freedom from people-pleasing

*Am I now trying to win the approval of human beings,
or of God? Or am I trying to please people? If I were still
trying to please people, I would not be a servant of Christ.*
GALATIANS 1:10 NIV

God calls us to be people-lovers not people-pleasers. We can love people wholeheartedly without losing ourselves in the process. Chronic people-pleasers tend to have these traits:
- Deeply struggle with saying no
- Pretend to agree with things you don't really agree with
- Take on the full responsibility for how others feel
- Overburden themselves in order to be liked and accepted

Chances are, if you're a people-pleaser, you are a deeply kind and empathetic person. And yet, you are also inherently worthy of respect regardless of what you have to offer. The issue with people-pleasing and a lack of healthy boundaries is that it is actually fear disguised as sacrifice—fear of what someone might think about you, fear of rejection, or fear that others won't value you outside of your performance.

On the other hand, genuine love exists from a place of choice. When we make choices from a reactive state of fear and image-control, we're likely not taking the time to think objectively about what's best for everyone involved—including ourselves. Practice pausing long enough to realign with your convictions and remember that God has called you to live in the spirit of freedom (II Corinthians 3:17).

I am capable of loving people wholeheartedly while staying in touch with my convictions and values.

HOW AM I FEELING TODAY?

☐ **1** Awful   ☐ **2** Poor   ☐ **3** Okay   ☐ **4** Good   ☐ **5** Great

LABELING:

Calm ————————————————————————— Anxious

Motivated ——————————————————————— Unmotivated

Loved ——————————————————————————Lonely

Happy——————————————————————————— Sad

Focused——————————————————————————Distracted

Grateful————————————————————————— Angry

HOURS OF SLEEP:

☐ 0 – 3   ☐ 4 – 6   ☐ 7 – 9   ☐ 10 – 12   ☐ 13+

EXERCISE: ☐ Yes   ☐ No

TOP 3 GOALS FOR TODAY:

1._____
2._____
3._____

3 THINGS I AM GRATEFUL FOR TODAY:

1._____
2._____
3._____

ONE PRACTICAL WAY I CAN APPLY TODAY'S READING:

_____
_____
_____
_____
_____
_____

the value of deep work

The beginning of wisdom is this:
Get wisdom, and whatever you get, get insight.
PROVERBS 4:7 ESV

In a world where we feel the constant temptation to prove ourselves publicly, remember that the most valuable growth is usually hidden. While the world obsesses over where we're going, God cares more about who we're becoming in the process. It's the development that comes during these unseen moments that ultimately bears fruit to what's seen in our lives and in our work. That often means slowing down, being more present-minded, and valuing what we're learning along the way. Whether it be on the job, in school, during a time of healing, or creating something new to put out into the world, what would life look like if your motivation was more learning-oriented instead of only outcome-focused? What if you dedicated this time to simply learn and apply what you know along the way? A life of less rigidity and more curiosity. A life of less proving and more growing.

This is where wisdom, which is priceless, comes from—learned experience. But remember, we often find wisdom in the hidden places. So normalize the idea that your process in the unseen is just as valuable, if not more valuable, than what's publicized.

I choose to live a life of less proving and instead value my growth process in the unseen.

DATE:_____

HOW AM I FEELING TODAY?

☐ **1** Awful ☐ **2** Poor ☐ **3** Okay ☐ **4** Good ☐ **5** Great

LABELING:

Calm ——————————————————————— Anxious

Motivated ——————————————————— Unmotivated

Loved ———————————————————————Lonely

Happy——————————————————————— Sad

Focused————————————————————Distracted

Grateful——————————————————————— Angry

HOURS OF SLEEP:

☐ 0 – 3 ☐ 4 – 6 ☐ 7 – 9 ☐ 10 – 12 ☐ 13+

EXERCISE: ☐ Yes ☐ No

TOP 3 GOALS FOR TODAY:

1._____
2._____
3._____

3 THINGS I AM GRATEFUL FOR TODAY:

1._____
2._____
3._____

ONE PRACTICAL WAY I CAN APPLY TODAY'S READING:

_____
_____
_____
_____
_____
_____

finding peace in clarity

For God is not a God of disorder but of peace,
as in all the meetings of God's holy people.

I CORINTHIANS 14:33 NLT

Sometimes an underlying feeling of anxiety comes from a lack of clarity. We may not be clear about what's expected of us, what our next steps should be, or what's been communicated to us. But instead of causing doubt, this anxiety can remind you to pause at any moment and respectfully ask questions until you are clear and have a sense of direction—not only from those around you but also from yourself.

There will always be things outside of our control that we can only surrender in faith. But gaining a better understanding of what's in our hands helps reduce stress and anxiety regarding the things within our control. Whether it be on the job, within a relationship, or any encounter we're still moving through with uncertainty, is there something in your life that's creating anxiousness simply because you're unclear about the situation? What would it practically look like to get clarity in this area so that you can walk in wisdom?

I am allowed to seek clarity from others to gain peace and direction to help guide my steps.

DATE:_____

HOW AM I FEELING TODAY?

☐ **1** Awful   ☐ **2** Poor   ☐ **3** Okay   ☐ **4** Good   ☐ **5** Great

LABELING:

Calm ————————————————————————— Anxious

Motivated ————————————————————— Unmotivated

Loved ——————————————————————— Lonely

Happy——————————————————————— Sad

Focused———————————————————————Distracted

Grateful———————————————————————— Angry

HOURS OF SLEEP:

☐ 0 – 3   ☐ 4 – 6   ☐ 7 – 9   ☐ 10 – 12   ☐ 13+

EXERCISE: ☐ Yes   ☐ No

TOP 3 GOALS FOR TODAY:

1._____
2._____
3._____

3 THINGS I AM GRATEFUL FOR TODAY:

1._____
2._____
3._____

ONE PRACTICAL WAY I CAN APPLY TODAY'S READING:

_____
_____
_____
_____
_____
_____

your mind is a temple

And now, dear brothers and sisters, one final thing.
Fix your thoughts on what is true, and honorable,
and right, and pure, and lovely, and admirable.
Think about things that are excellent
and worthy of praise.

PHILIPPIANS 4:8 NLT

The Bible says that your body is a temple, but have you considered your mind as a part of this temple? How would your relationship with your thoughts change if you truly saw your mind as a temple—a sacred space worthy of intentional care, nurturance, and surrender?

You take your mind with you everywhere you go. How you interpret and respond to the people, events, and interactions around you is translated through your mind. This is why our thought life is worth paying attention to. But the health of our minds is also made up of what we're feeding it.

Reflect on what has been allowed constant access to your mind that may have contributed to your feelings and attitudes this week: whether that positively or negatively impacted you, or simply drained you. And give yourself grace. It's natural to live on autopilot, especially when life feels overwhelming.

I invite you to use this moment to reclaim your mind and decide: What does it practically look like to care for this temple that you're living in every day?

My mind is a temple worthy of intentional care to live from a rooted place.

DATE:_____

HOW AM I FEELING TODAY?

☐ **1** Awful ☐ **2** Poor ☐ **3** Okay ☐ **4** Good ☐ **5** Great

LABELING:

Calm ————————————————————— Anxious

Motivated ————————————————— Unmotivated

Loved ——————————————————————Lonely

Happy——————————————————————— Sad

Focused———————————————————————Distracted

Grateful———————————————————————— Angry

HOURS OF SLEEP:

☐ 0 – 3 ☐ 4 – 6 ☐ 7 – 9 ☐ 10 – 12 ☐ 13+

EXERCISE: ☐ Yes ☐ No

TOP 3 GOALS FOR TODAY:

1. _____
2. _____
3. _____

3 THINGS I AM GRATEFUL FOR TODAY:

1. _____
2. _____
3. _____

ONE PRACTICAL WAY I CAN APPLY TODAY'S READING:

_____
_____
_____
_____
_____
_____

Immanuel: God with us

Fear not, for I am with you; be not dismayed,
for I am your God; I will strengthen you,
I will help you, I will uphold you
with my righteous right hand.

ISAIAH 41:10 ESV

When God declares "Fear not" from generation to generation, the phrase is repeatedly paired with a reassurance of God's presence and His faithfulness to see us through some of the most daunting trials of our lives.

"Fear not" appears so often throughout Scripture that the expression reasonably affirms that coming face-to-face with fear and anxiety has always been a part of the human experience and that God is there assuring us of His care for us every step of the way.

In the grips of anxiety, the brain's primary motive is survival. However, these responses are also psychosomatic: how your mind activates your body. Repeating messages of safety to yourself can help your mind integrate a sense of security back into your brain and body. Take a deep breath, with your hands on your chest, feeling the rhythm of your breath while speaking over yourself:

"Thank you for doing all you can to protect me, but I'm safe."

"I know this is triggering something similar to what I've been through before, but I'm choosing to take one step at a time and trust my ability to adapt to the outcome."

"God is with me; I will not fear."

When I am
afraid, I put
my trust in you.

PSALM 56:3 NIV

DATE:_____

HOW AM I FEELING TODAY?

☐ **1** Awful   ☐ **2** Poor   ☐ **3** Okay   ☐ **4** Good   ☐ **5** Great

LABELING:

Calm ——————————————————————— Anxious

Motivated —————————————————————— Unmotivated

Loved ——————————————————————— Lonely

Happy——————————————————————— Sad

Focused——————————————————————— Distracted

Grateful——————————————————————— Angry

HOURS OF SLEEP:

☐ 0 – 3   ☐ 4 – 6   ☐ 7 – 9   ☐ 10 – 12   ☐ 13+

EXERCISE: ☐ Yes   ☐ No

TOP 3 GOALS FOR TODAY:

1._____
2._____
3._____

3 THINGS I AM GRATEFUL FOR TODAY:

1._____
2._____
3._____

ONE PRACTICAL WAY I CAN APPLY TODAY'S READING:

_____
_____
_____
_____
_____
_____

the science of renewing your mind

Do not be conformed to this world, but be transformed by the renewal of your mind, that by testing you may discern what is the will of God, what is good and acceptable and perfect.

ROMANS 12:2 ESV

If practice makes perfect, what thoughts have you perfected by repeating them to yourself constantly? These are becoming your automatic thought patterns.

In the brain, renewing your mind literally means creating new, stronger neural pathways. This process is called *neuroplasticity*. You can think of it as trying to pave a new path through solid ground. The more you tread through this new path and create deeper tracks, the easier it will become to identify and walk down that path. Like building muscle, the more we strengthen certain pathways in the brain through practice, the easier it is to access those pathways.

In that same light, as we adapt to practicing healthier ways of thinking, new thought patterns can become a more consistent way of life for us. Today, as a simple practice, I encourage you to make note of a negative thought that typically comes up for you and write down at least two alternative ways to think about it. Sometimes just opening your mind to another option can help with perspective. It doesn't mean that we'll have perfect thinking, but it does mean that we can move through life differently and that there is real hope for getting better at renewing our minds.

I can pause
and practice a
different response
to renew my
thought patterns.

HOW AM I FEELING TODAY?

☐ **1** Awful   ☐ **2** Poor   ☐ **3** Okay   ☐ **4** Good   ☐ **5** Great

LABELING:

Calm ——————————————————————— Anxious

Motivated ————————————————————— Unmotivated

Loved ——————————————————————Lonely

Happy—————————————————————— Sad

Focused————————————————————Distracted

Grateful————————————————————— Angry

HOURS OF SLEEP:

☐ 0 – 3   ☐ 4 – 6   ☐ 7 – 9   ☐ 10 – 12   ☐ 13+

EXERCISE: ☐ Yes ☐ No

TOP 3 GOALS FOR TODAY:

1._____
2._____
3._____

3 THINGS I AM GRATEFUL FOR TODAY:

1._____
2._____
3._____

ONE PRACTICAL WAY I CAN APPLY TODAY'S READING:

_____
_____
_____
_____
_____
_____

you are
worthy of support

Share each other's burdens,
and in this way obey the law of Christ.

GALATIANS 6:2 NLT

Do you find it easy or difficult to allow yourself to be supported by those around you? Sometimes we become so focused on how we need to show up for others or how we want others to view us that we distance ourselves from being fully seen and supported in return. Maybe we've believed that because something is "our burden," it's up to us to fix ourselves. We don't want to be judged. We don't want others to witness our flaws. We think it will disqualify us in some way.

But if we're deeply honest, it's a control issue. We want to control how others view us— or we want to be seen as always in control. We've built all our worth into our performance. But it's in the safety of trusted friends and wise counsel that we can take a breath and be reminded that we are also worthy of love, support, and the grace to grow. Because you are worthy. This week I challenge you to be open to a safe relationship, fully as yourself.

I am worthy of being supported and allowed the grace to grow.

DATE: _____

HOW AM I FEELING TODAY?

☐ **1** Awful   ☐ **2** Poor   ☐ **3** Okay   ☐ **4** Good   ☐ **5** Great

LABELING:

Calm ————————————————————————— Anxious

Motivated ————————————————————— Unmotivated

Loved ———————————————————————— Lonely

Happy ————————————————————————— Sad

Focused————————————————————————Distracted

Grateful———————————————————————— Angry

HOURS OF SLEEP:

☐ 0 – 3   ☐ 4 – 6   ☐ 7 – 9   ☐ 10 – 12   ☐ 13+

EXERCISE: ☐ Yes   ☐ No

TOP 3 GOALS FOR TODAY:

1. _____
2. _____
3. _____

3 THINGS I AM GRATEFUL FOR TODAY:

1. _____
2. _____
3. _____

ONE PRACTICAL WAY I CAN APPLY TODAY'S READING:

_____

_____

_____

_____

_____

_____

release the weight of the world

*I have said these things to you, that in me you may
have peace. In the world you will have tribulation.
But take heart; I have overcome the world.*

JOHN 16:33 ESV

When the world feels overwhelming, divided, and hopeless with constant bad news, remember that it's okay to take a mental break. Too much negative media has been known to exacerbate our mental health, which doesn't serve anyone well in the end. We were never meant to carry all the world's problems on our own, and drawing boundaries around your media intake doesn't make you less concerned.

It's easy to react, as emotions rise and fall with every breaking story, but it takes intentionality and discernment to take a step back, align with our convictions, and understand what we can do to shift our focus and energy toward sowing where we are called to in this world. And that role will look different for everyone. First Corinthians 12:14–15 reminds us that "the body has many different parts, not just one part. If the foot says, 'I am not a part of the body because I am not a hand,' that does not make it any less a part of the body" (NLT). You are no less because you choose to act with intention—instead of reaction—by focusing on the areas in which you're most effective.

So take care of yourself, stay rooted, and sow what it is that you want to see more of in the world, starting by example in the ways that are true to you.

I am allowed
to pause and
reclaim my mind
to gain clarity
about how I'm
to respond to the
world around me.

HOW AM I FEELING TODAY?

☐ **1** Awful   ☐ **2** Poor   ☐ **3** Okay   ☐ **4** Good   ☐ **5** Great

LABELING:

Calm ————————————————————————— Anxious

Motivated ————————————————————— Unmotivated

Loved ——————————————————————————Lonely

Happy———————————————————————————— Sad

Focused—————————————————————————Distracted

Grateful———————————————————————— Angry

HOURS OF SLEEP:

☐ 0 – 3   ☐ 4 – 6   ☐ 7 – 9   ☐ 10 – 12   ☐ 13+

EXERCISE: ☐ Yes   ☐ No

TOP 3 GOALS FOR TODAY:

1._____
2._____
3._____

3 THINGS I AM GRATEFUL FOR TODAY:

1._____
2._____
3._____

ONE PRACTICAL WAY I CAN APPLY TODAY'S READING:

_____
_____
_____
_____
_____
_____

freedom from the bondage of opinions

So we can confidently say, "The Lord is my helper;
I will not fear; what can man do to me?"

HEBREWS 13:6 ESV

The moment we start obsessing over our every word, action, and appearance because we are concerned whether people will like us is the moment we become slaves to changing opinions. We'll never be at peace with ourselves while constantly shape-shifting in order to be accepted by every single person we come into contact with. Friend, we can't control people's personal preferences. When you live as who you're created to be, you will connect with the right people.

In today's world, you'll find an "amen" corner for every perspective and a critic for every position. Opinions don't hold up half as much as the convictions we live up to. Ask yourself this: "What keeps me rooted in who I am when the applause isn't there?" In other words, what are your reasons for what you do when the recognition isn't instant? Let *these* reasons be the foundation for why you show up, rather than fleeting validations.

Now, the attitude of "I don't care what anyone thinks!" is not a balanced way of approaching this. There is safety in an abundance of counselors (Proverbs 11:14). Those who genuinely come from a place of honesty and have our best interest at heart are voices to consider. As long as we are acting in integrity, all we can do is our personal best and trust God with the rest.

I accept that I can't control what people think of me, and I choose to focus on who I'm called to be.

DATE:_____

HOW AM I FEELING TODAY?

☐ **1** Awful   ☐ **2** Poor   ☐ **3** Okay   ☐ **4** Good   ☐ **5** Great

LABELING:

Calm ——————————————————————— Anxious

Motivated ——————————————————— Unmotivated

Loved ———————————————————————Lonely

Happy——————————————————————— Sad

Focused——————————————————————Distracted

Grateful——————————————————————— Angry

HOURS OF SLEEP:

☐ 0 – 3   ☐ 4 – 6   ☐ 7 – 9   ☐ 10 – 12   ☐ 13+

EXERCISE: ☐ Yes   ☐ No

TOP 3 GOALS FOR TODAY:

1._____
2._____
3._____

3 THINGS I AM GRATEFUL FOR TODAY:

1._____
2._____
3._____

ONE PRACTICAL WAY I CAN APPLY TODAY'S READING:

_____
_____
_____
_____
_____
_____

you are more than what you have to offer

If we are faithless, He remains faithful,
for He cannot disown Himself.
II TIMOTHY 2:13 NIV

How wonderful it is to know that God's faithfulness isn't dependent on our feelings—even when we feel faithless or burnt out. No matter where circumstances have brought you today, His love is wide enough, constant enough, and stable enough to carry you through your changing days. He cares for the state of your mind and soul beyond the state of your performance.

In a world that operates primarily on transactions, it can be difficult to fathom that there are things that aren't based solely on what we have to offer. While culture tells us we are as valuable as what we do, history has shown that the world will keep going regardless of our efforts. So who we are and how we show up through this life must transcend what we do.

Let it sink in that your worth was never dependent on your level of productivity. You are still worthy when you rest or take time to heal or take a step back to regather yourself. Ephesians 1:4 says that you were securely loved and chosen before the foundation of the earth. You were deemed worthy of love and belonging before you ever did a single thing—and you still are.

I am just as worthy in my resting as I am in my doing.

HOW AM I FEELING TODAY?

☐ **1** Awful　　☐ **2** Poor　　☐ **3** Okay　　☐ **4** Good　　☐ **5** Great

LABELING:

Calm ————————————————————————— Anxious

Motivated ——————————————————————— Unmotivated

Loved ——————————————————————————Lonely

Happy———————————————————————— Sad

Focused——————————————————————————Distracted

Grateful—————————————————————————— Angry

HOURS OF SLEEP:

☐ 0 – 3　　☐ 4 – 6　　☐ 7 – 9　　☐ 10 – 12　　☐ 13+

EXERCISE:　☐ Yes　☐ No

TOP 3 GOALS FOR TODAY:

1._____
2._____
3._____

3 THINGS I AM GRATEFUL FOR TODAY:

1._____
2._____
3._____

ONE PRACTICAL WAY I CAN APPLY TODAY'S READING:

_____
_____
_____
_____
_____
_____

responding versus reacting

But the fruit of the Spirit is love, joy, peace, patience, kindness, goodness, faithfulness, gentleness, self-control; against such things there is no law.
GALATIANS 5:22–23 ESV

We now live in a world infiltrated by hyperreactivity: reactions in comments, 140-character comebacks, and digital soapboxes at the click of a button. Social media has fostered a culture of reactivity to the point that it's a daily lifestyle right in the palm of our hands. But there's something to be said about the difference between *reacting* and *responding*.

Reacting can instantly rob our peace, lack self-control, and sometimes leave us with unintended consequences. *Responding* is the pause we take for our adrenaline to subside so we can make sound judgments, actively listen, be thoughtful about our intentions, or ultimately decide if something is even worth a response.

Today, remember that you have been given the spirit of self-control and a sound mind (II Timothy 1:7). You are a separate individual with your own thoughts, convictions, and emotions. Instead of enmeshing with every attitude or opinion that presents itself, allow yourself the in-between space for your own process by practicing emotional boundaries. You can even give yourself a prompting of "It's interesting that they feel this way about this. How do I feel about this? Is it worth engaging?" and reclaim your mind.

I have been given the spirit of self-control and a sound mind.

HOW AM I FEELING TODAY?

☐ **1** Awful   ☐ **2** Poor   ☐ **3** Okay   ☐ **4** Good   ☐ **5** Great

LABELING:

Calm ————————————————————————— Anxious

Motivated ————————————————————— Unmotivated

Loved ————————————————————————Lonely

Happy————————————————————————— Sad

Focused————————————————————————Distracted

Grateful———————————————————————— Angry

HOURS OF SLEEP:

☐ 0 – 3   ☐ 4 – 6   ☐ 7 – 9   ☐ 10 – 12   ☐ 13+

EXERCISE: ☐ Yes   ☐ No

TOP 3 GOALS FOR TODAY:

1._____
2._____
3._____

3 THINGS I AM GRATEFUL FOR TODAY:

1._____
2._____
3._____

ONE PRACTICAL WAY I CAN APPLY TODAY'S READING:

_____
_____
_____
_____
_____
_____

reframing stress

For You, O God, have tested us;
You have refined us like silver.
PSALM 66:10 BSB

What if I told you that not all stress is bad stress and not all pressure is bad pressure? There's a positive type of stress that challenges us to grow called *eustress*. Eustress is just enough pressure to motivate us to act beyond our comfort zones, which leads to the positive growth that benefits us in the end.

While a deadline, goal, test, or new undertaking may feel like an uncomfortable pressure, it can also be a necessary type of pressure, because without it, after a while we may become idle, apathetic, unmotivated, and unfulfilled. It goes to say that if we're not being challenged in some aspect of our lives, then we're probably not growing.

The difference between chronic stress and eustress is that chronic stress depletes our overall well-being and can have lasting negative effects, while eustress motivates us to expand beyond ourselves and can be exciting once accomplished. It brings us to life.

While some levels of pressure might feel uncomfortable at first, remember that discomfort isn't always a bad thing. So let's reframe this today. Are there any challenges in your life that seem like stressors but might actually be eustress and beneficial for you in the end?

I embrace challenges as opportunities to help me grow into my potential.

HOW AM I FEELING TODAY?

☐ **1** Awful   ☐ **2** Poor   ☐ **3** Okay   ☐ **4** Good   ☐ **5** Great

LABELING:

Calm ——————————————————————— Anxious

Motivated —————————————————— Unmotivated

Loved ———————————————————————Lonely

Happy——————————————————————— Sad

Focused————————————————————————Distracted

Grateful———————————————————————— Angry

HOURS OF SLEEP:

☐ 0 – 3   ☐ 4 – 6   ☐ 7 – 9   ☐ 10 – 12   ☐ 13+

EXERCISE: ☐ Yes   ☐ No

TOP 3 GOALS FOR TODAY:

1._____
2._____
3._____

3 THINGS I AM GRATEFUL FOR TODAY:

1._____
2._____
3._____

ONE PRACTICAL WAY I CAN APPLY TODAY'S READING:

_____
_____
_____
_____
_____
_____

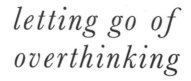

letting go of overthinking

So don't worry about tomorrow,
for tomorrow will bring its own worries.
Today's trouble is enough for today.

MATTHEW 6:34 NLT

Have you been overthinking and getting yourself worked up with something that is completely out of your hands? You can't control what someone else is thinking, you can't control someone else's choices, you can't control what happened in the past, and usually you can't control the timing or results of how events will play out.

Worrying about things like this only makes you feel worse while having no effect on the situation. You may believe if you ruminate on what's happening long enough, you'll somehow regain some control. And if you're ruminating from a place of worry, your perspective is already tainted by fear. So instead, mentally shift and take a deep breath. Identify and mentally release the things that you have no control over today into God's hands. Consider making a list of what those things are. No matter the outcome, God has you securely in the palm of His hand and He will never leave or forsake you. Faith is not the belief that everything will go as you picture; it's the belief that God has you no matter how things turn out.

Today I focus on the things that I can control and release the things outside of my control.

HOW AM I FEELING TODAY?

☐ **1** Awful   ☐ **2** Poor   ☐ **3** Okay   ☐ **4** Good   ☐ **5** Great

LABELING:

Calm ———————————————————— Anxious

Motivated ———————————————— Unmotivated

Loved ————————————————————Lonely

Happy——————————————————— Sad

Focused————————————————————Distracted

Grateful———————————————————— Angry

HOURS OF SLEEP:

☐ 0 – 3   ☐ 4 – 6   ☐ 7 – 9   ☐ 10 – 12   ☐ 13+

EXERCISE: ☐ Yes   ☐ No

TOP 3 GOALS FOR TODAY:

1._____
2._____
3._____

3 THINGS I AM GRATEFUL FOR TODAY:

1._____
2._____
3._____

ONE PRACTICAL WAY I CAN APPLY TODAY'S READING:

_____
_____
_____
_____
_____

bringing calm to your body

*My flesh and my heart may fail, but God is the
strength of my heart and my portion forever.*
PSALM 73:26 ESV

Anxiety is often not only in our heads but also experienced in our bodies. The nervous system plays a key role in the brain-body connection. So learning to partner with our bodies to regulate our nervous systems can help reduce the immediate physical feelings of anxiety. Specifically, stimulating the vagus nerve has been found to help bring feelings of calm back to the body. There are several ways you can stimulate your vagus nerve:

- Breath work through deep and slow belly breathing
- Cold exposure by taking a brief thirty-second cold shower or immersing your face in cold water to decrease your heart rate
- Prayer and meditation
- Movement: dance, exercise, and literally shaking it off
- Humming, singing, and gargling can help activate the vagus nerve, which is connected to your vocal cords
- Massaging specific pressure point areas gently, such as right behind your earlobes, around the curve of your ears, both sides of your neck right below the jawline, and your feet

God can bless us with many options to utilize out of a toolbox of resources for our well-being.

Let all that I am wait quietly before God, for my hope is in Him.

PSALM 62:5 NLT

HOW AM I FEELING TODAY?

☐ **1** Awful   ☐ **2** Poor   ☐ **3** Okay   ☐ **4** Good   ☐ **5** Great

LABELING:

Calm ——————————————————————— Anxious

Motivated ——————————————————— Unmotivated

Loved ————————————————————————Lonely

Happy ———————————————————————— Sad

Focused—————————————————————Distracted

Grateful——————————————————————— Angry

HOURS OF SLEEP:

☐ 0 – 3   ☐ 4 – 6   ☐ 7 – 9   ☐ 10 – 12   ☐ 13+

EXERCISE: ☐ Yes   ☐ No

TOP 3 GOALS FOR TODAY:

1._____
2._____
3._____

3 THINGS I AM GRATEFUL FOR TODAY:

1._____
2._____
3._____

ONE PRACTICAL WAY I CAN APPLY TODAY'S READING:

_____
_____
_____
_____
_____
_____

staying grounded through financial difficulty

*I know how to live on almost nothing or
with everything. I have learned the secret of living in
every situation, whether it is with a full stomach
or empty, with plenty or little.*

PHILIPPIANS 4:12 NLT

The moment you tie your identity to your finances is the moment you've placed your worth on shaky ground. Let's be honest: money is necessary to operate in this world, and it's stressful when we lack access to the resources we want and need. Also, nothing is wrong with having goals to generate more money. But your financial status still does not define the whole of you.

Money comes and goes throughout this life. When you tie your worth to your bank account, your esteem comes and goes with it. So decide to rebuild your foundation today. Learn to separate the two—your finances and who you are as a person. Your character, your gifts, and the potential you have to offer in this world stand apart from your current net worth.

I believe the person who is truly free can exist separately from material status—a person who is able to say, "Whether I have or don't have, I can stand in who I am. I know Whose I am, and I understand what matters most in this life. Anything else is an added blessing." Where have you been placing your identity lately?

My financial situation does not define the person I've been called and created to be in this world.

DATE:_____

HOW AM I FEELING TODAY?

☐ **1** Awful   ☐ **2** Poor   ☐ **3** Okay   ☐ **4** Good   ☐ **5** Great

LABELING:

Calm ————————————————————— Anxious

Motivated ——————————————————— Unmotivated

Loved ———————————————————————Lonely

Happy————————————————————————— Sad

Focused——————————————————————Distracted

Grateful———————————————————————— Angry

HOURS OF SLEEP:

☐ 0 – 3   ☐ 4 – 6   ☐ 7 – 9   ☐ 10 – 12   ☐ 13+

EXERCISE: ☐ Yes   ☐ No

TOP 3 GOALS FOR TODAY:

1._____
2._____
3._____

3 THINGS I AM GRATEFUL FOR TODAY:

1._____
2._____
3._____

ONE PRACTICAL WAY I CAN APPLY TODAY'S READING:

_____
_____
_____
_____
_____
_____

leaning into healthy conflict

Instead, we will speak the truth in love,
growing in every way more and more like Christ,
who is the head of His body, the church.

EPHESIANS 4:15 NLT

Would you consider yourself conflict-avoidant or resolution-forward? We tend to believe it's the things that are said that can cause the most harm to a relationship. But consider that oftentimes it's what's *unsaid* that leaves a relationship in ambiguity, disconnection, and resentment. We are wired for healthy attachment in relationship with others. So it's understandable when a difficult relationship or lingering issue creates underlying anxiety and disrupts our peace.

When we're able to lovingly and respectfully lay our concerns out on the table, it opens the opportunity to authentically work through our relationships in honesty. It also shows us the strength of that relationship. Sometimes it's in the friction that two people can be brought closer, sparking a new fire in the relationship.

Most times, resolving a conflict will feel uncomfortable before there's relief. Remind yourself that it's a part of the growth process that also strengthens our character. What isn't addressed will often repeat itself. So think about the long-term strength of the relationship. If you feel convicted to bring clarity and understanding into a relationship, consider first writing out your own thoughts on the matter so you have clarity from yourself when you do.

Facing conflict is a part of the growth process that is also strengthening my character.

DATE:_____

HOW AM I FEELING TODAY?

☐ **1** Awful   ☐ **2** Poor   ☐ **3** Okay   ☐ **4** Good   ☐ **5** Great

LABELING:

Calm ———————————————————————————— Anxious

Motivated ——————————————————————— Unmotivated

Loved ——————————————————————————Lonely

Happy—————————————————————————— Sad

Focused————————————————————————Distracted

Grateful——————————————————————— Angry

HOURS OF SLEEP:

☐ 0 – 3   ☐ 4 – 6   ☐ 7 – 9   ☐ 10 – 12   ☐ 13+

EXERCISE: ☐ Yes   ☐ No

TOP 3 GOALS FOR TODAY:

1. _____
2. _____
3. _____

3 THINGS I AM GRATEFUL FOR TODAY:

1. _____
2. _____
3. _____

ONE PRACTICAL WAY I CAN APPLY TODAY'S READING:

_____
_____
_____
_____
_____
_____

walking by faith

For we walk by faith, not by sight.

II CORINTHIANS 5:7 ESV

When deciding to step out and show up for something new, what if instead of seeing the feeling of anxiety as something to fear, you saw it as your body preparing you with the energy you need to take on a new challenge? This is called *cognitive reframing*. It's when you shift your ability to see a situation in a different way, which could actually turn out to be beneficial for you.

When we step into something new without knowing what the outcome will be, it's understandable that uncertainty and fear can get the best of us. However, it's also true that getting the different results that we want in our lives means doing something different than we're used to. It means challenging our own self-imposed limits to grow past where we've been. The upside is that we may end up in a different position than we ever thought was possible for ourselves because we took the chance. If nothing else, we learn how to improve upon our experiences for the next time.

Sometimes growth means feeling the fear and doing it anyway, because the temporary discomfort of change will far outweigh the constant struggles of keeping things the same. What's worth it to you?

I am able to feel uncomfortable feelings and still press forward toward the other side of my growth.

HOW AM I FEELING TODAY?

☐ **1** Awful ☐ **2** Poor ☐ **3** Okay ☐ **4** Good ☐ **5** Great

LABELING:

Calm ——————————————————————— Anxious

Motivated ——————————————————— Unmotivated

Loved ——————————————————————Lonely

Happy——————————————————————— Sad

Focused———————————————————————Distracted

Grateful——————————————————————— Angry

HOURS OF SLEEP:

☐ 0 – 3 ☐ 4 – 6 ☐ 7 – 9 ☐ 10 – 12 ☐ 13+

EXERCISE: ☐ Yes ☐ No

TOP 3 GOALS FOR TODAY:

1._____
2._____
3._____

3 THINGS I AM GRATEFUL FOR TODAY:

1._____
2._____
3._____

ONE PRACTICAL WAY I CAN APPLY TODAY'S READING:

_____
_____
_____
_____
_____
_____

showing up for your gifts

No one lights a lamp and then puts it under a basket.
Instead, a lamp is placed on a stand,
where it gives light to everyone in the house.

MATTHEW 5:15 NLT

Today is a reminder to show up for the gifts you've been given and the skills you've gained. Too often we convince ourselves to shrink and withdraw out of a false sense of humility that's really driven by the fear of being seen. Pause and reflect on the honest reasons you may be holding yourself back. You may find it has less to do with your capabilities or avoidance of vanity and more to do with the fear of exposure once you've decided to show up fully in your gifts.

Because the truth is that when we suppress our strengths, we suppress the potential to truly add to the lives of others, and we suppress the fulfillment we gain from operating in the ways we were wired to thrive. Conversely, it's when we're faithful in our gifts that we can give glory to our Creator.

You can confidently and actively participate in your skills while humbly being willing to learn and act in faith and integrity. Trust that you are capable of finding this balance.

I give myself permission to show up fully for my gifts.

HOW AM I FEELING TODAY?

☐ **1** Awful ☐ **2** Poor ☐ **3** Okay ☐ **4** Good ☐ **5** Great

LABELING:

Calm ————————————————————— Anxious

Motivated ———————————————————— Unmotivated

Loved ———————————————————————Lonely

Happy———————————————————————— Sad

Focused—————————————————————————Distracted

Grateful————————————————————————— Angry

HOURS OF SLEEP:

☐ 0 – 3   ☐ 4 – 6   ☐ 7 – 9   ☐ 10 – 12   ☐ 13+

EXERCISE: ☐ Yes ☐ No

TOP 3 GOALS FOR TODAY:

1._____
2._____
3._____

3 THINGS I AM GRATEFUL FOR TODAY:

1._____
2._____
3._____

ONE PRACTICAL WAY I CAN APPLY TODAY'S READING:

_____
_____
_____
_____
_____
_____

rest in the timing of your life

Trust in the LORD with all your heart,
and do not lean on your own understanding.

PROVERBS 3:5 ESV

When you begin to feel anxious or despair about the timing of your life in comparison to others, remember that God has seen every moment of your life laid out before a single day has passed (Psalm 139:16). He is entirely aware of the time.

When God has a plan for you, He doesn't need to check the timelines of those around you for confirmation about what He knows He's doing in *your* life. So keep your eyes forward. Remember, His ways are not our ways. He says, "For as the heavens are higher than the earth, so are my ways higher than your ways and my thoughts than your thoughts" (Isaiah 55:9 ESV).

The real problem is that we try to use earthly "accomplishments" or "status" to define ourselves. We think, *If I only have this, then it will prove, to myself and the world, that I am worth something.* Friend, you don't have to prove anything. Resist placing your security in comparing yourself with others (who don't have to live with your choices) and giving people and circumstances the power to define who you are. God is just getting started with you.

I choose to be
present in the
purposes of my life
even when things
look different from
the lives of those
around me.

DATE:_____

HOW AM I FEELING TODAY?

☐ **1** Awful   ☐ **2** Poor   ☐ **3** Okay   ☐ **4** Good   ☐ **5** Great

LABELING:

Calm ——————————————————————— Anxious

Motivated ——————————————————— Unmotivated

Loved ——————————————————————Lonely

Happy——————————————————————— Sad

Focused———————————————————————Distracted

Grateful——————————————————————— Angry

HOURS OF SLEEP:

☐ 0 – 3   ☐ 4 – 6   ☐ 7 – 9   ☐ 10 – 12   ☐ 13+

EXERCISE: ☐ Yes   ☐ No

TOP 3 GOALS FOR TODAY:

1._____

2._____

3._____

3 THINGS I AM GRATEFUL FOR TODAY:

1._____

2._____

3._____

ONE PRACTICAL WAY I CAN APPLY TODAY'S READING:

_____

_____

_____

_____

_____

conversations of the heart

This is My command—be strong and courageous!
Do not be afraid or discouraged.
For the LORD your God is with you wherever you go.

JOSHUA 1:9 NLT

Do you know who listens to you more than anyone in this world? You do. What you say to yourself in pivotal moments can be the most important words you'll say.

What makes a pivotal moment is not only what happens to us but how we respond to what's happened to us. This is why two people can experience the same event but approach it differently. Two people can feel the same fear and struggle with the same doubts, but while one speaks discouraging words to themselves, the other steps out in faith and faces the discomfort as part of the growth process.

They're both experiencing the same feelings, but they speak to themselves differently. This leads to different actions and different outcomes for how they're showing up for their lives. *But the good news is, any one of us can choose to speak faith over ourselves*. With practice, we can change the trajectory of how we speak to ourselves when it matters most.

David was a great example of facing reality while affirming truth to himself in the face of doubt: "Though an army encamp against me, my heart shall not fear; though war arise against me, yet I will be confident" (Psalm 27:3 ESV).

Today, literally place your hand on your heart and speak truth into your own soul.

I release my limiting beliefs to step into all that God has called me to be.

HOW AM I FEELING TODAY?

☐ **1** Awful   ☐ **2** Poor   ☐ **3** Okay   ☐ **4** Good   ☐ **5** Great

LABELING:

Calm ——————————————————————— Anxious

Motivated ————————————————— Unmotivated

Loved ———————————————————————Lonely

Happy——————————————————————— Sad

Focused———————————————————————Distracted

Grateful——————————————————————— Angry

HOURS OF SLEEP:

☐ 0 – 3   ☐ 4 – 6   ☐ 7 – 9   ☐ 10 – 12   ☐ 13+

EXERCISE: ☐ Yes   ☐ No

TOP 3 GOALS FOR TODAY:

1._____
2._____
3._____

3 THINGS I AM GRATEFUL FOR TODAY:

1._____
2._____
3._____

ONE PRACTICAL WAY I CAN APPLY TODAY'S READING:

_____
_____
_____
_____
_____
_____

getting clear about your emotions

As a face is reflected in water,
so the heart reflects the real person.

PROVERBS 27:19 NLT

Today, try to normalize seeing emotions as information. When we view our emotions as the enemy or as inconveniences in our lives and block them out completely, we disconnect ourselves from the same feedback system that is meant to inform us about our convictions, our deepest needs, and our areas in need of healing.

Being overwhelmed may mean we've lost sight of our priorities and need better boundaries. Anger may mean we're not being heard or have been violated in a way that needs our attention (or protection). Frustration may mean we've hit an obstacle that needs a different approach. Loneliness may mean we're lacking the human connection we were made for. Every emotion exists to serve a purpose, and God created us with emotions for a reason.

How we act on those emotions is where we're called to use discernment so we don't let our feelings rule us or define us. But self-awareness, partnered with these emotional indicators, can ultimately move us toward internal growth and emotional maturity. This may lead us to prayer or on a healing journey with a trusted counselor or toward taking the necessary steps to better align with our convictions and boundaries. What need might the root of your emotions be pointing you toward today?

I choose to make decisions from a place of emotional awareness instead of emotional reaction.

HOW AM I FEELING TODAY?

☐ **1** Awful   ☐ **2** Poor   ☐ **3** Okay   ☐ **4** Good   ☐ **5** Great

LABELING:

Calm ——————————————————————— Anxious

Motivated ——————————————————— Unmotivated

Loved ——————————————————————— Lonely

Happy ———————————————————————— Sad

Focused—————————————————————— Distracted

Grateful————————————————————— Angry

HOURS OF SLEEP:

☐ 0 – 3   ☐ 4 – 6   ☐ 7 – 9   ☐ 10 – 12   ☐ 13+

EXERCISE: ☐ Yes   ☐ No   .

TOP 3 GOALS FOR TODAY:

1._____
2._____
3._____

3 THINGS I AM GRATEFUL FOR TODAY:

1._____
2._____
3._____

ONE PRACTICAL WAY I CAN APPLY TODAY'S READING:

_____
_____
_____
_____
_____
_____

managing your expectations

And we know that for those
who love God all things work together for good,
for those who are called according to his purpose.

ROMANS 8:28 ESV

When something has turned out differently than we hoped, ruminating on the cycle of "should haves" can keep us stuck in a past that we can't change.

"I should have said this . . ."

"I should have done this differently . . ."

"Things should have gone this way . . ."

Reflecting on how our situation led to where it is can absolutely help us learn how to approach things differently the next time. However, there comes a time when you must decide to stop and shift your thoughts from the way things "should have" gone to what's happening in front of you now.

We are allowed the time and space to process and grieve the disappointment of how things could have been. Yet after a while, the tighter we cling to the imagined picture in our heads, when things have actually changed, the more hopeless we feel and the harder it is to mentally move forward. The more we allow ourselves to be adaptable to changes and manage our expectations, the more able we are to cope and make the most of our present reality.

What "should have" situation have you been holding on to? Is it time to surrender things and move forward?

When things haven't gone as planned, I am capable of adapting to my present reality.

HOW AM I FEELING TODAY?

☐ **1** Awful   ☐ **2** Poor   ☐ **3** Okay   ☐ **4** Good   ☐ **5** Great

LABELING:

Calm ————————————————————— Anxious

Motivated ——————————————— — Unmotivated

Loved ——————————————————Lonely

Happy—————————————— —— Sad

Focused———————————————Distracted

Grateful——————————————— Angry

HOURS OF SLEEP:

☐ 0 – 3   ☐ 4 – 6   ☐ 7 – 9   ☐ 10 – 12   ☐ 13+

EXERCISE: ☐ Yes   ☐ No

TOP 3 GOALS FOR TODAY:

1. _____
2. _____
3. _____

3 THINGS I AM GRATEFUL FOR TODAY:

1. _____
2. _____
3. _____

ONE PRACTICAL WAY I CAN APPLY TODAY'S READING:

_____

_____

_____

_____

_____

_____

understanding your own capacity

Be sure you know the condition of your flocks,
give careful attention to your herds.

PROVERBS 27:23 NIV

When the busyness of the day feels overwhelming and it seems like a million things are on your plate, remember that not everything that's demanding your attention is an automatic priority. The quickest way to lose our grounding is by letting too many outside demands crowd out the most important priorities.

Remember, nobody understands the context of your circumstances better than you, so it's up to you to define your capabilities for others.

Ultimately, we are human with limited time and limited capacity in a single day, so give yourself permission to set realistic expectations for yourself. Boundaries protect what matters most so we can walk in clarity and integrity. Consider:

Which responsibilities are time sensitive and which ones have a little more time flexibility?

What projects can be broken up into small tasks, accomplished one day at a time?

Are you able to provide other resources or solutions if something is outside of your capacity?

And friend, have respect for who and where you are. Each of our capacities will look different depending on our lifestyle. There's no guilt or shame in staying true to what's healthy for you.

I choose to be intentional rather than reactive to everything that demands my time and to give careful attention to what matters most.

DATE:_____

HOW AM I FEELING TODAY?

☐ **1** Awful   ☐ **2** Poor   ☐ **3** Okay   ☐ **4** Good   ☐ **5** Great

LABELING:

Calm ————————————————————————— Anxious

Motivated ——————————————————————— Unmotivated

Loved ———————————————————————— Lonely

Happy —————————————————————————— Sad

Focused———————————————————————— Distracted

Grateful———————————————————————— Angry

HOURS OF SLEEP:

☐ 0 – 3   ☐ 4 – 6   ☐ 7 – 9   ☐ 10 – 12   ☐ 13+

EXERCISE: ☐ Yes   ☐ No

TOP 3 GOALS FOR TODAY:

1._____

2._____

3._____

3 THINGS I AM GRATEFUL FOR TODAY:

1._____

2._____

3._____

ONE PRACTICAL WAY I CAN APPLY TODAY'S READING:

_____

_____

_____

_____

_____

_____

let God order your steps

Trust in the LORD with all your heart
and lean not on your own understanding;
in all your ways submit to Him,
and He will make your paths straight.

PROVERBS 3:5–6 NIV

Even when you don't know exactly where your life will lead, every experience up to this point is valuable. As you show up faithfully with the responsibilities already in your hands, you create a solid foundation of skills and knowledge to carry over as a strength in the next opportunity of your life. Recognize how far you've come. Recognize how much you've grown compared to what you knew before. Understand that your time and dedication have not been in vain.

When we take what we already have and steward our surroundings well, we show ourselves that we have a mature foundation capable of carrying more. That doesn't mean that we need to do everything perfectly in order to grow forward. It does mean that your purpose isn't just in a far-off destination you have yet to reach. Your purpose lives throughout a constant, evolving journey, making the most of what's in front of you as you're being molded for the opportunities that come to be most aligned with who you are and where you're called to be. Be okay with this process. God can work *all* things together and will order your steps.

When I don't know what the future holds, I trust that God is holding my future.

HOW AM I FEELING TODAY?

☐ **1** Awful   ☐ **2** Poor   ☐ **3** Okay   ☐ **4** Good   ☐ **5** Great

LABELING:

Calm ———————————————————————— Anxious

Motivated ——————————————————— Unmotivated

Loved ——————————————————————Lonely

Happy ——————————————————— Sad

Focused————————————————————Distracted

Grateful——————————————————— Angry

HOURS OF SLEEP:

☐ 0 – 3   ☐ 4 – 6   ☐ 7 – 9   ☐ 10 – 12   ☐ 13+

EXERCISE: ☐ Yes   ☐ No

TOP 3 GOALS FOR TODAY:

1. _____
2. _____
3. _____

3 THINGS I AM GRATEFUL FOR TODAY:

1. _____
2. _____
3. _____

ONE PRACTICAL WAY I CAN APPLY TODAY'S READING:

_____
_____
_____
_____
_____

finding beauty in the mundane

Give thanks in all circumstances;
for this is the will of God in Christ Jesus for you.
I THESSALONIANS 5:18 ESV

In a world where social media can create a hyperreality version of our lives from the best and biggest moments, let's take a step back and renormalize the beauty in the mundane.

There is beauty in going home to those you love.

There is honor in consistent work and the character it builds (Colossians 3:23).

There is necessity in slowing down.

There is joy in the small moments that put smiles on our faces.

We have this tendency to habituate to our circumstances. We get used to the things that we once wished we'd have. The things that we once hoped and prayed for become overlooked. They become our norm.

Today, close your eyes and meditate on three things that you once hoped for that you now have. Bring those things or people back into your awareness, appreciate them, and then give thanks to God.

God cares for you and still has you, even when your life doesn't look like a constant highlight reel. It's up to us to recognize this with love, with patience, and with humility every day.

Today, I choose
to appreciate
the things
I tend
to overlook.

DATE:_____

HOW AM I FEELING TODAY?

☐ **1** Awful   ☐ **2** Poor   ☐ **3** Okay   ☐ **4** Good   ☐ **5** Great

LABELING:

Calm ———————————————————————— Anxious

Motivated ——————————————————————— Unmotivated

Loved ———————————————————————— Lonely

Happy ————————————————————————— Sad

Focused——————————————————————— Distracted

Grateful———————————————————————— Angry

HOURS OF SLEEP:

☐ 0 – 3   ☐ 4 – 6   ☐ 7 – 9   ☐ 10 – 12   ☐ 13+

EXERCISE: ☐ Yes   ☐ No

TOP 3 GOALS FOR TODAY:

1._____
2._____
3._____

3 THINGS I AM GRATEFUL FOR TODAY:

1._____
2._____
3._____

ONE PRACTICAL WAY I CAN APPLY TODAY'S READING:

_____
_____
_____
_____
_____
_____

the paradox of happiness

Not that I am speaking of being in need, for I have
learned in whatever situation I am to be content.

PHILIPPIANS 4:11 ESV

In our cultural obsession with the pursuit of happiness, we convince ourselves there is consistently another thing out there that will make our lives more fulfilling than what it is. However, the issue with this mentality is that it creates a pattern of seeing our life from a constant deficit that needs to be met. The idea of happiness has been taken from its natural temporary emotion to being sought after as a constant state of being. In fact, research has found that, compared to other cultures, Western cultures tend to place greater value on high-arousal positive states like excitement and intense joy.[1] While in reality, many of our days will be lived in a neutral state, and that's totally normal.

But we fall for something called an *impact bias*, which is the tendency to overestimate how much and how long something will impact us, while underestimating how much other things will actually dominate our focus by then.

By the time we get the house we wanted, we're then focused on sustaining the mortgage.

By the time we get the job we wanted, we're then focused on keeping up with the job.

While there's nothing wrong with having goals, we also have to be mindful of being so future-focused that we rush past appreciating what we have at this point. What do you need to pause and appreciate today?

---

1   Nangyeon Lim, "Cultural Differences in Emotion: East-West Differences in Emotional Arousal Level," Integrative Medicine Research (March 2016).

Instead of shaming myself for where I'm not, I choose to celebrate how far I've come.

HOW AM I FEELING TODAY?

☐ **1** Awful   ☐ **2** Poor   ☐ **3** Okay   ☐ **4** Good   ☐ **5** Great

LABELING:

Calm ———————————————————————— Anxious

Motivated ———————————————————— Unmotivated

Loved ————————————————————————Lonely

Happy———————————————————————— Sad

Focused———————————————————————Distracted

Grateful———————————————————————— Angry

HOURS OF SLEEP:

☐ 0 – 3   ☐ 4 – 6   ☐ 7 – 9   ☐ 10 – 12   ☐ 13+

EXERCISE: ☐ Yes   ☐ No

TOP 3 GOALS FOR TODAY:

1._____

2._____

3._____

3 THINGS I AM GRATEFUL FOR TODAY:

1._____

2._____

3._____

ONE PRACTICAL WAY I CAN APPLY TODAY'S READING:

_____

_____

_____

_____

_____

_____

the wisdom of your body

My health may fail, and my spirit may grow weak,
but God remains the strength of my heart;
he is mine forever.

PSALM 73:26 NLT

The human body contains a feedback system of basic needs. In fact, your body is sending you messages all the time, telling you the current state that you're in and what you need—more rest, a decent meal, hydration, movement and blood flow, human connection, the level of safety in your environment, or your automatic feelings about something that's happened.

Scripture consistently affirms that there is an internal life embodied within each of us (Proverbs 4:23; 27:19) and that what we're carrying on the inside is the root of what will manifest on the outside—in our choices, in our words, in our automatic reactions. And our bodies store it all.

But rarely were we taught to partner with our bodies as an immediate source of insight. When we distance ourselves from our bodies in busyness or shame, instead of leaning in with compassion and curiosity, we block out the feedback system that is meant to nurture us into connection with ourselves and our deepest needs.

Do you tend to take on a more dismissive or mindful approach when it comes to your body? Pause and consider making intentional time for at least one basic need today.

Today I choose to live in connection with my body and pay attention to what it needs.

HOW AM I FEELING TODAY?

☐ **1** Awful   ☐ **2** Poor   ☐ **3** Okay   ☐ **4** Good   ☐ **5** Great

LABELING:

Calm —————————————————————— Anxious

Motivated ———————————————————— Unmotivated

Loved ———————————————————————Lonely

Happy———————————————————————— Sad

Focused———————————————————————Distracted

Grateful——————————————————————— Angry

HOURS OF SLEEP:

☐ 0 – 3   ☐ 4 – 6   ☐ 7 – 9   ☐ 10 – 12   ☐ 13+

EXERCISE: ☐ Yes   ☐ No

TOP 3 GOALS FOR TODAY:

1._____
2._____
3._____

3 THINGS I AM GRATEFUL FOR TODAY:

1._____
2._____
3._____

ONE PRACTICAL WAY I CAN APPLY TODAY'S READING:

_____
_____
_____
_____
_____
_____

the mind-body connection

Give your burdens to the LORD,
and He will take care of you.

PSALM 55:22 NLT

Practicing mindfulness can simply mean that we are pausing, refocusing on the present, checking in with our bodies, reengaging our senses, and also learning how to sit with uncomfortable feelings by letting them pass through like a wave. Use this intentional time of pausing to release a prayer over yourself. Breathe in and exhale: "I know the LORD is always with me. I will not be shaken, for He is right beside me" (Psalm 16:8 NLT).

This is considered a bottom-up approach: self-regulating the body first and then working toward the mind. Having a regular practice of intentional stillness and deep relaxation techniques for twenty to thirty minutes daily can lead to an overall more regulated state. This has also been evidentially shown to improve overall focus and attention.[2]*

With your hands resting on your abdomen, practice ten sets of a full, deep inhale through your nose, slowly counting to four, then exhaling through your mouth to a count of four, and letting your body and limbs loosen completely. You should feel your abdomen doing most of the expanding.

Today, consider engaging breathing techniques in a moment of overwhelm to help pause and shift your mind and body into a cooldown mode.

---

2   Adam Moore, Thomas Gruber, Jennifer Derose, and Peter Malinowsk, "Regular, Brief Mindfulness Meditation Practice Improves Electrophysiological Markers of Attentional Control," Frontiers in Human Neuroscience, 6, 18 (February 10, 2012).

The LORD is always with me. I will not be shaken, for He is right beside me.

PSALM 16:8 NLT

DATE:_____

HOW AM I FEELING TODAY?

☐ **1** Awful   ☐ **2** Poor   ☐ **3** Okay   ☐ **4** Good   ☐ **5** Great

LABELING:

Calm ———————————————————————— Anxious

Motivated ———————————————————— Unmotivated

Loved ——————————————————————Lonely

Happy——————————————————————— Sad

Focused—————————————————————Distracted

Grateful———————————————————— Angry

HOURS OF SLEEP:

☐ 0 – 3   ☐ 4 – 6   ☐ 7 – 9   ☐ 10 – 12   ☐ 13+

EXERCISE: ☐ Yes   ☐ No

TOP 3 GOALS FOR TODAY:

1._____
2._____
3._____

3 THINGS I AM GRATEFUL FOR TODAY:

1._____
2._____
3._____

ONE PRACTICAL WAY I CAN APPLY TODAY'S READING:

_____
_____
_____
_____
_____
_____

resetting a hard day

Therefore do not worry about tomorrow,
for tomorrow will worry about itself.
Each day has enough trouble of its own.
MATTHEW 6:34 NIV

Today, it's okay if all you can focus on are the twenty-four hours in front of you—and let tomorrow deal with tomorrow. When the day looks overwhelming, instead of ruminating about the entire day, break your day down into quarters. For example, 8:00–10:00 a.m. (first quarter), 11:00 a.m.–1:00 p.m. (second quarter), 2:00–3:00 p.m. (third quarter), and 4:00–5:00 p.m. (fourth quarter)—or whichever times best suit your lifestyle. Then dedicate yourself to a single task in each quarter. Coming up with a practical and simplified plan for your day encourages proactive behavior that can help you feel unstuck.

Now, if your morning got off to a rough start in the first quarter, that's okay. You can take a deep breath, let that first quarter go, and start over again in the second quarter. You can do the same in the third quarter and fourth quarter, over and over if you have to. The key to tackling overwhelming days is to keep your mind present as each hour comes. And at any point, give yourself permission to pause, to set aside the rush for one moment of stillness, and to surrender the big picture into God's hands.

You will keep
in perfect peace
all who trust in
You, all whose
thoughts are
fixed on You!

ISAIAH 26:3 NLT

HOW AM I FEELING TODAY?

☐ **1** Awful   ☐ **2** Poor   ☐ **3** Okay   ☐ **4** Good   ☐ **5** Great

LABELING:

Calm ——————————————————————— Anxious

Motivated ——————————————————— Unmotivated

Loved ——————————————————————Lonely

Happy———————————————————————— Sad

Focused——————————————————————Distracted

Grateful——————————————————————— Angry

HOURS OF SLEEP:

☐ 0 – 3   ☐ 4 – 6   ☐ 7 – 9   ☐ 10 – 12   ☐ 13+

EXERCISE: ☐ Yes   ☐ No

TOP 3 GOALS FOR TODAY:

1._____
2._____
3._____

3 THINGS I AM GRATEFUL FOR TODAY:

1._____
2._____
3._____

ONE PRACTICAL WAY I CAN APPLY TODAY'S READING:

_____
_____
_____
_____
_____
_____

your identity versus your feelings

And when I wake up, You are still with me!

PSALM 139:18 NLT

There is nothing in this world that provides us more security than knowing we are in the palm of God's hand at all times.

It's so easy to define ourselves by the ups and downs of our days. But the truth is that we are who He says we are in spite of how we feel about ourselves. Wholeheartedly loved. Eternally secure. Wonderfully made. Called out and set apart for a purpose. God's love is consistent and exists independent of our changing moods.

Today, be reminded that your identity and your feelings are two separate things.

Who you are and what you feel are two separate things.

On hard days, you are still loved.

On unproductive days, you still have purpose.

On imperfect days, you are still worthy of belonging.

On anxious days, you're still His.

He has you. Rest in this truth today.

My feelings and my identity are two separate things. My feelings may change, but who I'm called to be remains the same.

DATE:_____

HOW AM I FEELING TODAY?

☐ **1** Awful   ☐ **2** Poor   ☐ **3** Okay   ☐ **4** Good   ☐ **5** Great

LABELING:

Calm ——————————————————————— Anxious

Motivated ——————————————————— Unmotivated

Loved ——————————————————————Lonely

Happy———————————————————————— Sad

Focused———————————————————————Distracted

Grateful——————————————————————— Angry

HOURS OF SLEEP:

☐ 0 – 3   ☐ 4 – 6   ☐ 7 – 9   ☐ 10 – 12   ☐ 13+

EXERCISE: ☐ Yes   ☐ No

TOP 3 GOALS FOR TODAY:

1._____
2._____
3._____

3 THINGS I AM GRATEFUL FOR TODAY:

1._____
2._____
3._____

ONE PRACTICAL WAY I CAN APPLY TODAY'S READING:

_____
_____
_____
_____
_____
_____

letting go of perfectionism

*And I am sure of this, that he who began
a good work in you will bring it to completion
at the day of Jesus Christ.*
PHILIPPIANS 1:6 ESV

The reason we hold on to perfectionism is because it serves us. While perfectionism completely holds us back, it also keeps us in a "safe" place where we'll never be seen—therefore never risking failure or criticism.

The problem with perfectionism is that it doesn't allow you to be a beginner in anything. It requires the unrealistic expectation that you'll be a finished product without any of the showing up that builds the experience that grows you forward.

But we all have to start somewhere. We all have to experiment a bit to see what works for us and learn from what doesn't work. So let yourself be a part of the learning process rather than depending so strictly on validation. Human acceptance comes and goes, but the growth journey outlives opinions.

The more we focus on ourselves, the more we hear the voice of our doubts. But the more we focus on God's greater work and love for creation, the more we see where His grace meets our weakness and realize that all of this isn't relying on our perfection. Give yourself permission to start where you are, as you are, and remember God's grace is sufficient to see you through.

I can feel vulnerable and show up anyway, while learning from my experiences.

DATE:_____

HOW AM I FEELING TODAY?

☐ **1** Awful   ☐ **2** Poor   ☐ **3** Okay   ☐ **4** Good   ☐ **5** Great

LABELING:

Calm —————————————————————————— Anxious

Motivated —————————————————————— Unmotivated

Loved ——————————————————————————Lonely

Happy —————————————————————————— Sad

Focused—————————————————————————Distracted

Grateful————————————————————————— Angry

HOURS OF SLEEP:

☐ 0 – 3   ☐ 4 – 6   ☐ 7 – 9   ☐ 10 – 12   ☐ 13+

EXERCISE: ☐ Yes   ☐ No

TOP 3 GOALS FOR TODAY:

1._____
2._____
3._____

3 THINGS I AM GRATEFUL FOR TODAY:

1._____
2._____
3._____

ONE PRACTICAL WAY I CAN APPLY TODAY'S READING:

_____
_____
_____
_____
_____
_____

reframing the
comparison trap

Pay careful attention to your own work, for then you
will get the satisfaction of a job well done, and you
won't need to compare yourself to anyone else.

GALATIANS 6:4 NLT

Comparison happens naturally, many times without thinking. If you've ever put down your phone feeling worse than you did when you picked it up, then you've likely been there. Your thoughts toward yourself become more doubtful. You find yourself more frustrated. You begin to feel behind and discontent with your place in life. It's all very implicit—a subtle arrest of your mind and spirit, stealing your contentment, your peace, and your sense of self.

Comparison is a trap because in either way we apply it, it never leads to a healthy outcome. With upward comparisons, we overestimate others and underestimate ourselves. With downward comparisons, we place others as less than ourselves to compensate for voids of insecurity. It's counterproductive in the long run. So instead, try asking yourself, "What is it that's drawing me to this person? Is it their work ethic, their willingness to take risks, their boldness of conviction, their skill level?" Then consider how these may simply be areas you admire and want to improve in while embracing your own individual differences.

Today, remember you are most empowered in your calling, by growing in the way that God is shaping you according to your makeup and the purpose over your life.

I can admire what I see in others without discounting the work God is doing within me.

HOW AM I FEELING TODAY?

☐ **1** Awful ☐ **2** Poor ☐ **3** Okay ☐ **4** Good ☐ **5** Great

LABELING:

Calm ———————————————————— Anxious

Motivated ——————————————————— Unmotivated

Loved ———————————————————— Lonely

Happy ———————————————————— Sad

Focused ———————————————————— Distracted

Grateful ———————————————————— Angry

HOURS OF SLEEP:

☐ 0 – 3 ☐ 4 – 6 ☐ 7 – 9 ☐ 10 – 12 ☐ 13+

EXERCISE: ☐ Yes ☐ No

TOP 3 GOALS FOR TODAY:

1. _____
2. _____
3. _____

3 THINGS I AM GRATEFUL FOR TODAY:

1. _____
2. _____
3. _____

ONE PRACTICAL WAY I CAN APPLY TODAY'S READING:

_____
_____
_____
_____
_____
_____

creating conversation boundaries

But the wisdom from above is first pure,
then peaceable, gentle, open to reason, full of mercy
and good fruits, impartial and sincere.

JAMES 3:17 ESV

One of the biggest ways we sabotage our own peace is by allowing ourselves to become too enmeshed in the attitudes of others. For example, the quarrelsome person who has a patten of turning things into a heated argument with no resolve. This type of conversation has a pattern of being more harmful than helpful. It's fueled by pride instead of understanding (James 1:19), and it will mentally and emotionally drain you every time.

While you may not be able to completely avoid the individual, you are allowed to use wisdom to draw boundaries around conversations that bear no fruit. This is where the practice of setting emotional boundaries comes into play. It's separating the thoughts and feelings that are yours from the thoughts and feelings that belong to others.

There are many difficult conversations that are also very necessary to have to help bring about a solution. However, we're not talking about avoiding difficulty. We're talking about preserving your energy from fruitless conversations. Proverbs 26:4 NLT reminds us not to "answer the foolish arguments of fools, or you will become as foolish as they are."

Consider letting them know, "I hear what you're saying; however, this has a history of ending badly, so I'd rather not have these types of conversations. I hope that we can leave this on a respectful note."

I do not have
to take on the
attitudes that
don't belong to me.
Instead, I choose
to live in faith,
discernment, and
self-control.

DATE:_____

HOW AM I FEELING TODAY?

☐ **1** Awful   ☐ **2** Poor   ☐ **3** Okay   ☐ **4** Good   ☐ **5** Great

LABELING:

Calm ————————————————————— Anxious

Motivated ————————————————— Unmotivated

Loved ——————————————————————Lonely

Happy—————————————————————— Sad

Focused———————————————————Distracted

Grateful————————————————————— Angry

HOURS OF SLEEP:

☐ 0 – 3   ☐ 4 – 6   ☐ 7 – 9   ☐ 10 – 12   ☐ 13+

EXERCISE: ☐ Yes   ☐ No

TOP 3 GOALS FOR TODAY:

1._____
2._____
3._____

3 THINGS I AM GRATEFUL FOR TODAY:

1._____
2._____
3._____

ONE PRACTICAL WAY I CAN APPLY TODAY'S READING:

_____
_____
_____
_____
_____
_____

Jehovah Shalom: the God of peace

Now may the Lord of peace himself give you peace at all times in every way. The Lord be with you all.

II THESSALONIANS 3:16 ESV

Peace is the nature of God, and He invites us to let His peace wash over us so we can be refreshed in the stillness of His presence. When anxiety consumes our lives, sometimes we've lost sight of who God is. We get so buried in the bustle and the noise of the world that we stop surrendering our worries to Him and cling desperately to our own control. But we soon find that our own control is limited. All the while, God desires for us to experience living in a peace that transcends our circumstances, trusting that He is capable of doing infinitely more than we could ask or imagine (John 14:27; Ephesians 3:20). His presence isn't just a feeling, it's a promise to be with us always—whether we feel it or not.

We find peace in God's provision when we understand how much He loves us. Many of us don't truly know what safety looks like, let alone the safety of love. But our Father in heaven invites us to find this safety in Him, maybe for the first time ever, and be vulnerable enough to trust that His love is faithful to see us through all things.

No matter how far away you feel, as you surrender your heart and continue to seek Him, He will draw near to you (James 4:8).

I trust that
God is with me
regardless of how
I feel.

DATE:_____

HOW AM I FEELING TODAY?

☐ **1** Awful   ☐ **2** Poor   ☐ **3** Okay   ☐ **4** Good   ☐ **5** Great

LABELING:

Calm ——————————————————————— Anxious

Motivated ——————————————————— Unmotivated

Loved ———————————————————————Lonely

Happy——————————————————————— Sad

Focused————————————————————————Distracted

Grateful——————————————————————— Angry

HOURS OF SLEEP:

☐ 0 – 3   ☐ 4 – 6   ☐ 7 – 9   ☐ 10 – 12   ☐ 13+

EXERCISE: ☐ Yes   ☐ No

TOP 3 GOALS FOR TODAY:

1._____
2._____
3._____

3 THINGS I AM GRATEFUL FOR TODAY:

1._____
2._____
3._____

ONE PRACTICAL WAY I CAN APPLY TODAY'S READING:

_____
_____
_____
_____
_____

strategies for overwhelm

*Give careful thought to the paths for your feet
and be steadfast in all your ways.*

PROVERBS 4:26 NIV

Isn't it ironic that whenever you find yourself in high-stress situations, everything seems to start going wrong at the same time? You're not alone there, friend. The truth is, stress is a part of life. Throughout this life, we're constantly presented with new pressures that challenge us out of our comfort zones. So stress management—having our own strategy for moving through stress—is a core life skill not only for our minds but also for our physical health and overall well-being.

When you feel overwhelmed by multiple problems at one time, start by making a list prioritizing your *most* distressing issue down to the *least* distressing issue. Try to get clear with yourself about what's affecting you the most right now. Then start addressing the things on your list one at a time. When you focus on dealing with the bigger issues first, it will bring more relief for you to work your way down toward focusing on the smaller issues.

You may have to set more boundaries to focus on resolving core issues and take things off your plate in the areas that you can. Once your foundation is more stable, then you'll feel more at ease about carrying on with the usual aspects of life. Remember, peace is not just the absence of problems but learning how to ground our minds and souls through our problems.

My help comes
from the LORD,
the Maker of
heaven and
earth.

PSALM 121:2 NIV

DATE:_____

HOW AM I FEELING TODAY?

☐ **1** Awful   ☐ **2** Poor   ☐ **3** Okay   ☐ **4** Good   ☐ **5** Great

LABELING:

Calm ———————————————————————— Anxious

Motivated ———————————————————— Unmotivated

Loved ————————————————————————Lonely

Happy———————————————————————— Sad

Focused————————————————————————Distracted

Grateful———————————————————————— Angry

HOURS OF SLEEP:

☐ 0 – 3   ☐ 4 – 6   ☐ 7 – 9   ☐ 10 – 12   ☐ 13+

EXERCISE: ☐ Yes ☐ No

TOP 3 GOALS FOR TODAY:

1._____
2._____
3._____

3 THINGS I AM GRATEFUL FOR TODAY:

1._____
2._____
3._____

ONE PRACTICAL WAY I CAN APPLY TODAY'S READING:

_____
_____
_____
_____
_____

finding soul-rest

And he said, "My presence will go with you,
and I will give you rest."

EXODUS 33:14 ESV

When we're not operating from an internally secure and grounded place, we soon find ourselves hustling for our worth from external approval and burning out in the process.

Burn out can look like:

- Feeling impatient and short-tempered with people
- Feeling overwhelmed and forgetful
- Feeling inadequate and unaccomplished
- Losing a sense of personal boundaries and resenting your commitments
- Mental and physical exhaustion
- Growing physically sick

It can be easy to misplace our worth in our work, in how much we can produce, or in how valuable we are to others. There's a natural aspect to it. To thrive, we all need a level of self-efficacy, some level of confidence in our abilities. But when we begin to feel like no amount of what we do or level of what we become is ever enough, striving for more and more validation becomes exhausting and impossible to fulfill.

Friend, the work will always be there to return to. People will always be around. The world will keep going, but there is only one of you. So, take care of yourself. At some point, you have to let your efforts be enough. Take a step back to reassess your boundaries, realign with your priorities, and make time for the things that bring rest and joy to your soul. And know that God-given worth isn't something you achieve—it's something you carry.

God-given worth isn't something you achieve— it's something you carry.

DATE:_____

HOW AM I FEELING TODAY?

☐ **1** Awful ☐ **2** Poor ☐ **3** Okay ☐ **4** Good ☐ **5** Great

LABELING:

Calm ————————————————————————— Anxious

Motivated ——————————————————————— Unmotivated

Loved ———————————————————————————Lonely

Happy——————————————————————————— Sad

Focused ——————————————————————————Distracted

Grateful———————————————————————— Angry

HOURS OF SLEEP:

☐ 0 – 3   ☐ 4 – 6   ☐ 7 – 9   ☐ 10 – 12   ☐ 13+

EXERCISE: ☐ Yes ☐ No

TOP 3 GOALS FOR TODAY:

1._____
2._____
3._____

3 THINGS I AM GRATEFUL FOR TODAY:

1._____
2._____
3._____

ONE PRACTICAL WAY I CAN APPLY TODAY'S READING:

_____
_____
_____
_____
_____
_____

where faith
meets wisdom

If you need wisdom, ask our generous God,
and He will give it to you.
He will not rebuke you for asking.

JAMES 1:5 NLT

If God is the source of wisdom and knowledge, then God is also the source of common sense, practicality, and discernment (Proverbs 2:6). When it comes to making decisions, understand that having faith and using practical wisdom aren't opposites. In fact, Proverbs 4:7 reminds us that "getting wisdom is the wisest thing you can do! And whatever else you do, develop good judgment" (NLT).

I believe that God is fully capable of giving us wisdom and confirmation on what path to take for our lives. But there are also many times when we have to make hard decisions, knowing that in either way that we choose, He can work all things together for good in the end. So when you're stuck on whether you're making the perfect decision or you're unsure of what God is leading you to do, lean on both prayer and sound judgment.

Consider making a list of the pros and cons for each choice you are faced with. Gather as much credible information as you can to help make an informed decision, and then honestly reflect on what each choice is worth to you. You are allowed the space to get with your convictions, get with wise and trusted people, and get with God to have faith for what is best for you (and possibly your dependents). Amen?

I can use practical wisdom and discernment as a part of making faith-filled decisions.

HOW AM I FEELING TODAY?

☐ **1** Awful   ☐ **2** Poor   ☐ **3** Okay   ☐ **4** Good   ☐ **5** Great

LABELING:

Calm ——————————————————————————— Anxious

Motivated ———————————————————————— Unmotivated

Loved ——————————————————————————— Lonely

Happy —————————————————————————— Sad

Focused ——————————————————————— Distracted

Grateful ——————————————————————— Angry

HOURS OF SLEEP:

☐ 0 – 3   ☐ 4 – 6   ☐ 7 – 9   ☐ 10 – 12   ☐ 13+

EXERCISE: ☐ Yes   ☐ No

TOP 3 GOALS FOR TODAY:

1._____
2._____
3._____

3 THINGS I AM GRATEFUL FOR TODAY:

1._____
2._____
3._____

ONE PRACTICAL WAY I CAN APPLY TODAY'S READING:

_____
_____
_____
_____
_____

flexibility is your friend

*Do not be anxious about anything, but in everything
by prayer and supplication with thanksgiving let your
requests be made known to God. And the peace of God,
which surpasses all understanding, will guard your
hearts and your minds in Christ Jesus.*

PHILIPPIANS 4:6–7 ESV

Do you consider yourself rigid or flexible when responding to changes in your day? It's upsetting when you have the day planned to go one way and it goes a different way, or when you have a set list of things you want to accomplish, but it just doesn't seem to get completely done. However, rigidity and having a tight grip on control actually ends up controlling your mind and spirit instead. Because the moment something unplanned pops up or you don't finish something as planned, you trap yourself in a cycle of shame and anxiety.

Many of us fall into a common mental bias called *the control fallacy*. You somehow believe that you should be able to control everything. But if you feel like you have to control everything, then it's likely that you tend to assume unrealistic responsibility and shame for things that are totally out of your hands.

Take a deep breath and realize that the more you feel the urge to control, the more it's a sign you need to surrender, because it has too great of a hold on you. And consider reflecting on your motives. What are you trying to prove and to whom? There is usually more than one way to reach a goal. Allow yourself options. Remember God is sovereign.

Today, I surrender my need for absolute control and trust God with the things I cannot change.

HOW AM I FEELING TODAY?

☐ **1** Awful   ☐ **2** Poor   ☐ **3** Okay   ☐ **4** Good   ☐ **5** Great

LABELING:

Calm ——————————————————————— Anxious

Motivated ——————————————————— Unmotivated

Loved ——————————————————————Lonely

Happy——————————————————————— Sad

Focused——————————————————————Distracted

Grateful——————————————————————— Angry

HOURS OF SLEEP:

☐ 0 – 3   ☐ 4 – 6   ☐ 7 – 9   ☐ 10 – 12   ☐ 13+

EXERCISE: ☐ Yes   ☐ No

TOP 3 GOALS FOR TODAY:

1. _____
2. _____
3. _____

3 THINGS I AM GRATEFUL FOR TODAY:

1. _____
2. _____
3. _____

ONE PRACTICAL WAY I CAN APPLY TODAY'S READING:

_____

_____

_____

_____

_____

_____

rethinking
imposter syndrome

The LORD will fulfill his purpose for me;
your steadfast love, O LORD, endures forever.
Do not forsake the work of your hands.

PSALM 138:8 ESV

Do you ever have a deep fear that people are going to find out that you're not as great at what you do as they think you are? Turns out you're not alone. And there's a word for it—it's called *imposter syndrome*.

Some signs of imposter syndrome include holding back out of fear of exposure, never feeling you've earned what you worked for, hustling to prove you belong, and dismissing your achievements and skills as luck.

Friend, this is your reminder that if you worked hard to get where you are, you are not an imposter. You are right where you're supposed to be, and you are effective. Your experience up to this point is valuable.

In fact, if you're experiencing imposter syndrome, then it more likely means that you're doing well enough for people to have noticed. Think about it. If you weren't doing well, then you wouldn't have anything to feel like an imposter about. So it's proof of the opposite of what you've believed. It's just your turn to see it!

And when you show up in *your* skin, all that you've brought along with your journey will show up with you, and it will be enough. So rest confidently in the providence of God as He carries you forward to fulfill the purposes in your life.

The LORD will
fulfill his
purpose for me.

PSALM 138:8 ESV

HOW AM I FEELING TODAY?

☐ **1** Awful   ☐ **2** Poor   ☐ **3** Okay   ☐ **4** Good   ☐ **5** Great

LABELING:

Calm ————————————————————————— Anxious

Motivated —————————————————————— Unmotivated

Loved ——————————————————————————Lonely

Happy——————————————————————————— Sad

Focused———————————————————————————Distracted

Grateful——————————————————————————— Angry

HOURS OF SLEEP:

☐ 0 – 3   ☐ 4 – 6   ☐ 7 – 9   ☐ 10 – 12   ☐ 13+

EXERCISE: ☐ Yes   ☐ No

TOP 3 GOALS FOR TODAY:

1._____
2._____
3._____

3 THINGS I AM GRATEFUL FOR TODAY:

1._____
2._____
3._____

ONE PRACTICAL WAY I CAN APPLY TODAY'S READING:

_____
_____
_____
_____
_____

fully known and fully loved

*Let us then approach God's throne of grace
with confidence, so that we may receive mercy
and find grace to help us in our time of need.*

HEBREWS 4:16 NIV

When you feel like it's impossible to consistently measure up to the ideal image you want for yourself, rest in the grace of God where you are fully known and fully loved as you are in this moment. Extend this same grace to yourself.

We call this the *real self* versus the *ideal self*. In this constant hustle to become someone other than who we are, we get hooked into this cycle of striving to prove ourselves. But God doesn't ask for your perfectly curated life, and He cares for your true self far more than any image. There's nothing about your life that takes Him by surprise. He made your heart, so He *understands* everything you do (Psalm 33:15). Let that sink in. The Lord is in touch with every feeling, every emotion, and every thought you have—which means you can always come to Him fully as yourself.

Today in prayer, bring Him your mess. Bring Him your unspoken worries. Bring Him your guarded insecurities. Surrender it all and live in the freedom of authenticity over perfection. And don't let reaching for an image make you lose sight of what you already have to appreciate and the core of who you're genuinely becoming in the process.

Today I choose rest in the security of being fully known and fully loved right where I am.

HOW AM I FEELING TODAY?

☐ **1** Awful ☐ **2** Poor ☐ **3** Okay ☐ **4** Good ☐ **5** Great

LABELING:

Calm ————————————————————————————— Anxious

Motivated ——————————————————————————— Unmotivated

Loved ———————————————————————————————Lonely

Happy————————————————————————————— Sad

Focused————————————————————————— Distracted

Grateful———————————————————————————— Angry

HOURS OF SLEEP:

☐ 0 – 3 ☐ 4 – 6 ☐ 7 – 9 ☐ 10 – 12 ☐ 13+

EXERCISE: ☐ Yes ☐ No

TOP 3 GOALS FOR TODAY:

1. _____
2. _____
3. _____

3 THINGS I AM GRATEFUL FOR TODAY:

1. _____
2. _____
3. _____

ONE PRACTICAL WAY I CAN APPLY TODAY'S READING:

_____
_____
_____
_____
_____
_____

strategies for coping with stress

Count it all joy, my brothers, when you meet trials of various kinds, for you know that the testing of your faith produces steadfastness.

JAMES 1:2–3 ESV

A large part of coping with stress is understanding what coping strategies you can use to gain the clarity you need to move forward. For example, we can choose to be emotion-focused or problem-focused.

Being *emotion-focused* is most helpful in situations where you're facing an issue that's outside of your control. Instead of fixating on the issue itself, you decide to shift your focus inward on how to help reduce the negative feelings you're having around the issue. This could be through surrendering your worries in prayer and worship, journaling, talking through things with someone, reframing how you choose to see the issue, movement and exercise, and so on. Being emotion-focused concentrates on how to regulate *yourself* within your circumstances.

Being *problem-focused* is most helpful in situations where the stressors are more controllable and you can actively do things that will help resolve the issue. In these situations, you help relieve stress and anxiety by tackling the problem head-on. This could mean working on better time management, increasing your studying or practice time, completing a task you've been putting off, or confronting a conflict you've been avoiding.

I am capable
of confronting
difficult situations
with patience for
myself and the
clarity to direct
my steps.

HOW AM I FEELING TODAY?

☐ **1** Awful   ☐ **2** Poor   ☐ **3** Okay   ☐ **4** Good   ☐ **5** Great

LABELING:

Calm ——————————————————————— Anxious

Motivated ———————————————————— Unmotivated

Loved ——————————————————————— Lonely

Happy ——————————————————————— Sad

Focused —————————————————————— Distracted

Grateful ——————————————————————— Angry

HOURS OF SLEEP:

☐ 0 – 3   ☐ 4 – 6   ☐ 7 – 9   ☐ 10 – 12   ☐ 13+

EXERCISE: ☐ Yes ☐ No

TOP 3 GOALS FOR TODAY:

1._____
2._____
3._____

3 THINGS I AM GRATEFUL FOR TODAY:

1._____
2._____
3._____

ONE PRACTICAL WAY I CAN APPLY TODAY'S READING:

_____
_____
_____
_____
_____
_____

a Biblical basis for boundaries

Each of you should give what you have decided in your heart to give, not reluctantly or under compulsion, for God loves a cheerful giver.

II CORINTHIANS 9:7 NIV

Ask yourself, "Just because I *can* do it, does it mean I *should*?" When we stretch ourselves thin by trying to be everything to everyone, naturally our priorities begin to fall out of place. If you're finding that some of the most important aspects of your life are slipping through your fingers because they're being crowded out by the demands of others, this can be a sign that you've disconnected from yourself and your convictions. We best serve others when our service comes from the clarity of a mentally and spiritually grounded place.

That also means knowing what you can't do so you can do the things you're called to do. It's important to stay in touch with God and the healthy intuitive convictions He's given you to live your life in a way that is authentic, honest, and sustainable. Sacrificing your mental and emotional health is neither more holy nor always more helpful in the long run. Choose mental, emotional, and spiritual health so you can show up wholeheartedly.

I am allowed to set the boundaries I need to best serve others from a mentally and spiritually grounded place.

DATE:_____

HOW AM I FEELING TODAY?

☐ **1** Awful ☐ **2** Poor ☐ **3** Okay ☐ **4** Good ☐ **5** Great

LABELING:

Calm ————————————————————— Anxious

Motivated ———————————————— Unmotivated

Loved ——————————————————— Lonely

Happy ———————————————————— Sad

Focused ——————————————————— Distracted

Grateful ———————————————————— Angry

HOURS OF SLEEP:

☐ 0 – 3   ☐ 4 – 6   ☐ 7 – 9   ☐ 10 – 12   ☐ 13+

EXERCISE: ☐ Yes ☐ No

TOP 3 GOALS FOR TODAY:

1. _____
2. _____
3. _____

3 THINGS I AM GRATEFUL FOR TODAY:

1. _____
2. _____
3. _____

ONE PRACTICAL WAY I CAN APPLY TODAY'S READING:

_____
_____
_____
_____
_____
_____

choosing faith over fear

*Do not be anxious about anything, but in everything
by prayer and supplication with thanksgiving let your
requests be made known to God. And the peace of God,
which surpasses all understanding, will guard your
hearts and your minds in Christ Jesus.*

PHILIPPIANS 4:6–7 ESV

D oes your mind tend to automatically jump to assuming the
worst possible outcome? *Catastrophizing* is exactly what
it sounds like—thinking the worst about situations that haven't
happened or don't exist. We fixate on the fearful situation that
we're convinced is *going* to happen, even when a number of
our fears don't play out as we've imagined.

Romans 8:6 (ESV) reminds us that "to set the mind on
the flesh is death, but to set the mind on the Spirit is life and
peace." Faith and fear both take mental energy; it's about which
one we'll choose to give our energy to. We can either search
our circumstances for ways to affirm our fear or trust that God
has us no matter the outcome, and then rest in a peace beyond
our current understanding.

While you may want to prepare your heart for any outcome,
know that you are more resilient than you may realize to adapt
to any challenge you face. You have done this many times. So
instead of occupying your mind replaying the worst possible
outcome, give yourself a mental break until you know more,
and trust that, should you need to, you can face things as they
come.

I will not let fear determine my future. God's plans are greater than my fears.

DATE:_____

HOW AM I FEELING TODAY?

☐ **1** Awful ☐ **2** Poor ☐ **3** Okay ☐ **4** Good ☐ **5** Great

LABELING:

Calm ———————————————————— Anxious

Motivated ———————————————————— Unmotivated

Loved ———————————————————— Lonely

Happy ———————————————————— Sad

Focused ———————————————————— Distracted

Grateful ———————————————————— Angry

HOURS OF SLEEP:

☐ 0 – 3   ☐ 4 – 6   ☐ 7 – 9   ☐ 10 – 12   ☐ 13+

EXERCISE: ☐ Yes ☐ No

TOP 3 GOALS FOR TODAY:

1._____
2._____
3._____

3 THINGS I AM GRATEFUL FOR TODAY:

1._____
2._____
3._____

ONE PRACTICAL WAY I CAN APPLY TODAY'S READING:

_____
_____
_____
_____
_____
_____

hold on to your anchors

Peace I leave with you; my peace I give to you.
Not as the world gives do I give to you.
Let not your hearts be troubled,
neither let them be afraid.

JOHN 14:27 ESV

When the waves of life feel as if they're crashing all around you, find your anchors and hold on to them as you ride out the storm. Think about it, what is an anchor? According to *Merriam-Webster*, an anchor is a "person or thing that provides strength and support." Your anchor keeps you tethered to a solid foundation so that you are unmovable no matter what waves are coming your way.

Some examples of holding on to anchors in life are having a therapist or counselor in your corner to turn to, sharing with a support group or trusted friends and family, using creative expression to cope, and leaning into prayer and Christ and His Word in times of despair. Pay attention to what's working in your life or what has worked to help keep your mind in the right place, and commit to prioritizing space for them regularly for your own good.

Reflect today and consider which anchors in your life keep your mind and soul grounded. How can you incorporate them into your life more?

I can't always control what happens to me, but I can control the type of person I choose to be.

DATE:_____

HOW AM I FEELING TODAY?

☐ **1** Awful   ☐ **2** Poor   ☐ **3** Okay   ☐ **4** Good   ☐ **5** Great

LABELING:

Calm ——————————————————————— Anxious

Motivated ——————————————————— Unmotivated

Loved ——————————————————————Lonely

Happy——————————————————————— Sad

Focused———————————————————————Distracted

Grateful——————————————————————— Angry

HOURS OF SLEEP:

☐ 0 – 3   ☐ 4 – 6   ☐ 7 – 9   ☐ 10 – 12   ☐ 13+

EXERCISE: ☐ Yes   ☐ No

TOP 3 GOALS FOR TODAY:

1._____
2._____
3._____

3 THINGS I AM GRATEFUL FOR TODAY:

1._____
2._____
3._____

ONE PRACTICAL WAY I CAN APPLY TODAY'S READING:

_____
_____
_____
_____
_____

grace for the process

Instead, let the Spirit
renew your thoughts and attitudes.
EPHESIANS 4:23 NLT

Relapsing into the grips of negative thought patterns happens to the best of us. So instead of shamefully asking yourself, "How am I back here again?" compassionately ask yourself, "What do I need right now to get my mind grounded?"

We often think, "I was in such a good place. I was doing well. I was just starting to feel good about myself again." And then *boom*—the right combination of circumstances can quickly trigger us into a downward spiral.

It's not about never having a negative thought again or being completely rid of trials. That's an unrealistic expectation. It's about understanding that life will be both—the peaks and the valleys—and finding your anchors along the way. It's understanding that you can always start over, no matter how far gone you feel.

So if you've found yourself in a relapse in your thinking today, instead of shaming yourself for where you are, use this moment as an indicator to begin asking yourself, "What do I need in order to take care of myself right now?" And have grace for yourself. No one is immune to the human experience. God will complete the work He has begun in you.

I can sit with difficult emotions to get clear about my true needs and grow in emotional maturity.

HOW AM I FEELING TODAY?

☐ **1** Awful   ☐ **2** Poor   ☐ **3** Okay   ☐ **4** Good   ☐ **5** Great

LABELING:

Calm ——————————————————————————— Anxious

Motivated ————————————————————— Unmotivated

Loved ————————————————————————Lonely

Happy———————————————————————— Sad

Focused——————————————————————Distracted

Grateful———————————————————————— Angry

HOURS OF SLEEP:

☐ 0 – 3   ☐ 4 – 6   ☐ 7 – 9   ☐ 10 – 12   ☐ 13+

EXERCISE: ☐ Yes   ☐ No

TOP 3 GOALS FOR TODAY:

1._____
2._____
3._____

3 THINGS I AM GRATEFUL FOR TODAY:

1._____
2._____
3._____

ONE PRACTICAL WAY I CAN APPLY TODAY'S READING:

_____
_____
_____
_____
_____
_____

look at how far you've come

Jesus replied, "You don't understand now what I am doing, but someday you will."

JOHN 13:7 NLT

Anxiety focuses on the outcome you don't know. Faith focuses on the faithfulness of God who knows you and has you. Where is your focus today?

Many people don't know what it took for you to get where you are today, but by the grace of God you got here. That may feel like some miracle. Sometimes we move so fast through life that we forget the obstacles we've faced and the battles we've already overcome.

Psalm 78:11 (ESV) speaks to future generations about the Israelites' deliverance from Egypt: "They forgot his works and the wonders that he had shown them." We, too, clouded by our present reality, forget that He has delivered us once before. He carried us through what felt impossible before, and that same care for us has never changed.

When you begin to feel doubts about your present situation, look at the track record of your past. Make a list of all the things you've overcome. You have survived 100 percent of your worries and fears, because God's plans are, and always will be, greater than your fears.

Sometimes having faith means letting go of every fear, doubt, and uncertainty to understand this one thing: God is faithful, and He cares for you.

God's faithfulness that has carried me this far will continue to carry me forward.

HOW AM I FEELING TODAY?

☐ **1** Awful ☐ **2** Poor ☐ **3** Okay ☐ **4** Good ☐ **5** Great

LABELING:

Calm ———————————————————————— Anxious

Motivated ——————————————————— Unmotivated

Loved ———————————————————————Lonely

Happy———————————————————————— Sad

Focused————————————————————————Distracted

Grateful———————————————————————— Angry

HOURS OF SLEEP:

☐ 0 – 3 ☐ 4 – 6 ☐ 7 – 9 ☐ 10 – 12 ☐ 13+

EXERCISE: ☐ Yes ☐ No

TOP 3 GOALS FOR TODAY:

1. _____

2. _____

3. _____

3 THINGS I AM GRATEFUL FOR TODAY:

1. _____

2. _____

3. _____

ONE PRACTICAL WAY I CAN APPLY TODAY'S READING:

_____

_____

_____

_____

_____

_____

about the author

BRITTNEY MOSES is a writer, speaker, advocate and psychology graduate of UCLA encouraging the integration of faith, holistic mental health, and wellness. From serving in churches over the past decade, formerly founding an international youth nonprofit ministry, and as a NAMI-certified support group facilitator, Brittney aspires to encourage those who are quietly wrestling in the shadows by bringing mental health issues into the light and making them accessible and relatable aspects of the national conversation. When she's not writing posts for her popular blog BrittneyMoses.com or hosting her Faith & Mental Wellness Podcast, Brittney can often be found hitting the California beaches and spending precious time with her son, Austin, and husband, Jason.

LIVE YOUR FAITH

Dear Friend,

This book was prayerfully crafted with you, the reader, in mind. Every word, every sentence, every page was thoughtfully written, designed, and packaged to encourage you—right where you are this very moment. At DaySpring, our vision is to see every person experience the life-changing message of God's love. So, as we worked through rough drafts, design changes, edits, and details, we prayed for you to deeply experience His unfailing love, indescribable peace, and pure joy. It is our sincere hope that through these Truth-filled pages your heart will be blessed, knowing that God cares about you—your desires and disappointments, your challenges and dreams.

He knows. He cares. He loves you unconditionally.

BLESSINGS!
THE DAYSPRING BOOK TEAM

**Additional copies of this book and
other DaySpring titles can be purchased
at fine retailers everywhere.
Order online at <u>dayspring.com</u>
or
by phone at 1-877-751-4347**